NOTES,

HISTORICAL AND BIBLIOGRAPHICAL,

ON THE

LAWS OF NEW HAMPSHIRE.

BY

ALBERT H. HOYT.

NOTES,

HISTORICAL AND BIBLIOGRAPHICAL,

ON THE

LAWS OF NEW HAMPSHIRE.

BY ALBERT H. HOYT.

"ANY GOVERNMENT IS FREE TO THE PEOPLE UNDER IT, WHATEVER BE THE FORM, WHERE THE LAWS RULE, AND THE PEOPLE ARE A PARTY TO THOSE LAWS."

CENTRAL EXCHANGE.
1876.

One hundred copies reprinted, from the "Proceedings of the American Antiquarian Society," for April, 1876, with additions.

HISTORICAL AND BIBLIOGRAPHICAL NOTES

ON THE

LAWS OF NEW HAMPSHIRE.

THE history of the origin and development of the Laws of New Hampshire deserves and could not fail to reward the most thorough investigation. Moreover, if the history of that State for the first eighty years is ever to be intelligently studied and correctly written such an investigation will be pre-requisite. For the purpose of calling fresh attention to this subject, and in the hope that some one may be led to undertake this work, the following Historical and Bibliographical Notes are submitted as a slight contribution to the end above proposed.

The early history of New Hampshire is still to a great degree involved in confusion and obscurity. The causes of this are obvious. Enough, however, of that history is known to enable us to take in its general outlines.

The colonization of the country of the "Pascataway," or Piscataqua, a part of which was afterward included in the larger territory known as New Hampshire, was a private commercial enterprise. There is no evidence that the patentees or grantees designed to provide an asylum for a discontented, disaffected, or persecuted people, or for such as felt themselves to be persecuted, or for any who were obnoxious to the laws of the realm. Nor is there the slightest evidence that at the outset of the enterprise its promoters even so much as dreamed of founding a self-governing State, or a community in any essential degree independent of the imperial sovereignty. They were loyal to the Crown and to the Church of England.

But as no scheme of this kind could be expected to succeed without local superintendents, so we find that this colony on the Piscataqua had its "governors,"—agents of the chief adventurers, and overseers of their interests. The first settlers, mostly servants in the employ of the grantees, were ruled by these overseers, under the instruction of their principals. All owed allegiance to and were governed by the laws of England.

As the population increased, and local causes began to operate, a more efficient government, involving a larger representation of interests, became both convenient and necessary. This necessity was the more pressing after Portsmouth and Dover became distinct centres of population.

In the absence of records, or other authentic evidence, it is impossible at present to fix the exact time when these two communities set up government for themselves, but it was at an earlier period, most likely, than has generally been assigned.

It is stated by some writers that the inhabitants of Portsmouth instituted a local government soon after the departure of Captain Walter Neale, Mr. Mason's steward, in 1633. By the word "inhabitants" they can mean only such of the settlers as had an interest in the soil, or were possessed of other considerable property. Reference is made in the Court Records to a certain "combination," or written plan of government, as early as 1643; but the first act of the people of Portsmouth, of which we have any record, that looks like a proceeding under a "combination," bears date May 25, 1640. Undoutedly, however, an orderly government had existed for several years.*

The settlers of Exeter, a community entirely distinct from those just mentioned, formed themselves into a body politic† on the 4th of July, 1639. Their example was followed by Dover on the 22d of October in the same year.‡ Whether their action was preceded or followed by that of Portsmouth is as yet uncertain.

* See the letter of the Rev. George Burdett to the Archbishop of Canterbury, of 29 Nov., 1638, in "Transcript of Original Documents relating to the Early History of New Hampshire," edited by John Scribner Jenness. New York, 1876.

† A fac-simile of the Exeter "Combination" is given in the "Wentworth Genealogy."

‡ For the Dover "Combination" entire, see Jenness's "Transcript of Orig. Documents," p. 36.

Hampton, which was claimed by Massachusetts Bay to be within its charter limits, accepted from that colony the rights and powers of a township in 1639.*

At this period the entire population of these districts did not much exceed, if it equalled, one thousand souls; and this number included all the people of whom we have any knowledge as then living or settled within what is now called New Hampshire. These people, like the colonists of Massachusetts Bay, belonged to the great middle class of Englishmen.

There is no evidence that prior to 1641, either Portsmouth or Dover had adopted a formal code of laws. Still, it is not to be inferred that these communities were lawless, or destitute of some kind of regulations for the conduct of their public affairs. They certainly had the laws and customs of England which they brought with them.

The settlers of Exeter, composed mainly of exiles from Massachusetts, did establish a body of laws, which, though in some respects repugnant to the laws of England, were, upon the whole, creditable to the intelligence and liberality of the man who framed them.†

In 1641, Portsmouth and Dover were brought under the jurisdiction of Massachusetts Bay, the way thereto having been prepared by the friends and agents of that colony.‡ Exeter, after the departure of Mr. Wheelwright, submitted two years later.

This extension of jurisdiction lasted until New Hampshire was erected into a royal Province, with a separate government, consisting of a President and Council and a House of Representatives. During this period of nearly forty years the people, though nominally subject to the laws of Massachusetts Bay, were really and in the main governed by their own local laws and magistrates.

The commission of President Cutt and his Council passed the great seals on the 18th of September, 1679, was delivered to him in person by Edward Randolph on the 30th of December, pub-

* Mass. Col. Records, I., 259.
† New Hamp. His. Soc. Coll., VI., 192.
‡ Ibid, (Centennial Address of the Hon. Jeremiah Smith); Winthrop II., 28, 38, 42, (1st ed.)

lished by the President, against the earnest opposition of two or three persons named therein as Councillors, early in January, 16$\frac{79}{80}$, and on the 21st of that month the new government went into operation.

Power was given to establish Courts, raise money for certain purposes by taxation and excise, and to raise, equip, and command a body of Militia. Instructions were also given to call an Assembly of the people, by delegates, who were authorized to make laws suitable to the wants of the people, but not repugnant to the Constitution and laws of England.

A General Assembly convened in Portsmouth March 16, 16$\frac{79}{80}$, and at this and subsequent sessions in that year framed and published a code of laws. This code comprised sixteen "capital," twenty-seven "criminal," and forty-five "general" laws. The following eleven crimes were made punishable with death, viz: idolatry, blasphemy, treason, wilful murther, manslaughter, murder, witchcraft, bestiality, buggery, false witness ("of purpose to take away a man's life"), and cursing of parents (by a son). The punishment of death, or "other grievous punishment," was affixed to six crimes, viz: public rebellion, manstealing, rebellion (by a son) against parents, rape, wilful burning of a house, barn, ship or bark, and burglary (on the third conviction).

Although the President and Council had received from the King a copy* of the Statutes of England, "copiously and accurately done," for their instruction and guidance, they do not seem to have had that "special regard" for it which they claimed in their Address to the King, under date of 11 June, 1680.†

It has been stated by different writers, and is generally believed, that this code was borrowed from the laws of Massachusetts Bay. This is an error; for, in fact, the entire criminal code, with the exception of a few sections and some slight verbal differences, was taken from the laws of the "Colony of New Plimouth."

By comparing the "Lawes and Libertyes" of Massachusetts, of 1641, 1660, and 1672, with this New Hampshire code, it will be seen that the latter makes a juster discrimination in the

* One volume then comprised all the laws of England!—Whitelocke on Parliamentary Writ.

† This and their previous Address, of 29 March, it is probable, were the work of that astute politician, the Rev. Joshua Moodey.

definition and classification of crimes and in the punishments prescribed. For instance: in the Massachusetts code adultery is punishable with death; in the New Hampshire, with whipping. In the former, public rebellion also is punishable with death; in the latter, with death, or "some other grievous punishment," in the discretion of the Court. The law against blasphemy, in the New Hampshire code, contains the important qualifying words, — "any person professing the true God;" and in the law against witchcraft, the qualifying words are, — "if any Christian, so called, be a witch," etc.

Courts of law, even in modern times, have found it to be almost an insoluble question as to what constitutes drunkenness. The law-makers of New Hampshire, copying from their brethren of New Plymouth, adopted the following comprehensive and simple definition, viz.: —

> "By drunkenness is to be understood one y[t] lisps or falters in his speech by reason of overmuch drinke, or y[t] staggers in his going, or y[t] vomits by reason of excessive drinking, or y[t] cannot, by reason thereof, follow his calling."

At this time, New Hampshire, like her neighbors, had neither newspapers nor newspaper reporters, but like them she had an excessive supply of mongers of false news, and retailers of malicious gossip. Her law, adopted in 1680 and kept upon the statute-book many years, but unfortunately now repealed, reads as follows: —

> "That w[t] p'rson soever, being 16 yeares of age, or upward, shall wittingly or willingly make or publish any lie w[ch] may be tending to y[e] damage or hurt of any p'ticular p'son, or wth intent to deceive and abuse y[e] people with false news or reports, shall be fined for every such default 10s., and if y[e] p'tie cannot, or will not, pay y[e] fine, then he shall sit in y[e] stocks as long as y[e] Court shall thinke meete; and if the offenders shall come to any one of Councill and own his offence, it shall be in y[e] power of any one of y[e] Councill afore[sd] to execute y[e] law upon him where he liveth, and spare his appearance at y[e] Court; but in case when y[e] lie is greatly p'nicious to y[e] Comon Weale, it shall be more severely punished, according to y[e] nature of it."

But even this severe and elastic law failed to effect a cure; and so twenty-two years afterward, in the 13th year of the reign of William III., the punishment was made more severe, and the lowest limit of the age of accountability under this statute was fixed at 14 instead of 16 years.

According to instructions, this code was transmitted to England, and, as we are informed by Chalmers, was totally disallowed in

December, 1681. That part of it which relates to crimes was first printed in 1831,* and the whole code was first printed in 1866.†

President Cutt, an "ancient and infirm man" when he was commissioned, who by reason of growing feebleness had taken but little part in the government, died on the 27th of March, 1682, and was succeeded by the Deputy, Richard Walderne, an energetic man and a zealous friend of Massachusetts. He was superseded by Edward Cranfield, whose commission as Lieutenant-Governor and Commander-in-Chief passed the seals May 9, 1682. By other commissions, from the Duke of York, bearing date 29 June, 1682, he was made Vice-Admiral, Judge, Register, and Marshal of the Admiralty for the Province, with power of appointing substitutes or deputies in said offices. By these commissions and his instructions, much greater powers were conferred upon Cranfield than had been granted to his predecessor.

Governor Cranfield landed in Salem October 1, 1682; proceeded to Portsmouth on the 3d, and on the next day took the oaths of office and published his commissions. On the 4th of November a General Assembly convened in Portsmouth, and adopted a new body of laws, twenty-five in number. These were first printed in 1866.‡ This code reduced the number of capital crimes, and, in several particulars, the punishments for offences of an inferior grade were made less severe. In some other respects it appears that the Assembly had profited by the fate of their previous attempt at law-making.

If it be true, as has been claimed by more than one philosophical writer, that the character of the criminal laws of a nation or community affords a true indication of its prosperity, intelligence and morality, the New England colonies, at this period of their history, will not suffer in comparison with the most enlightened nations of Europe of that day.

By the laws of Massachusetts, adopted in 1641, twelve crimes were declared to be capital; and, although this class of crimes was increased by subsequent enactments, yet early in the

---

* Farmer's Belknap (Appendix), 453-455.

† N. H. His. Soc. Coll., VIII., 9-35; Prov. Papers of N. H., I., 382-408 (pub. in 1867).

‡ N. H. His. Soc. Coll., VIII, 90-96.

last century we discover a continual tendency toward an amelioration of the penal code, and to a more rational distinction in the grades and punishments of offences of all kinds.

The New Plymouth Colony code of 1671, printed in 1672, and the same code as it stood in 1685, made thirteen crimes absolutely, and four more conditionally, punishable with death.

As we have seen, the New Hampshire code of 1680 enumerates eleven crimes for which the only punishment was death, and that the number of capital offences was reduced under Cranfield's administration. In 1718, the number was seven, and two more on second conviction for two other crimes. Since the Act of 19 June, 1812, the highest punishment, death, is confined to murder and treason.

In England, prior to the Commonwealth, the number of capital crimes, as fixed by statute, and as known to the common law was, it is said, not less than one hundred and fifty. This number was largely increased after the Restoration. In the 160 years between that event and the death of George III., 187 crimes more were added. By successive Acts, between 1824 and 1861, the number has been reduced to murder and treason.

To William Penn, however, belongs the praise that in his well-conceived and well-expressed code of 1682, he recognized only two capital crimes, — murder and treason; and in this, as in many other things, that wise man was nearly two hundred years in advance of his contemporaries.

There is one feature of both the Cutt and Cranfield commissions deserving of special reference. It is that article which recites, in unambiguous terms, the guaranty of religious liberty:—"We do hereby require and command that liberty of conscience shall be allowed unto all Protestants." That is, the same liberty and no more, which was allowed at that time to Protestant dissenters in England. But, assuming that the persons addressed knew that the Church of England was, by law, the Church of the King's Province, lest they should draw unauthorized conclusions from this concession, the king reminds them "that such especially as shall be conformable to the rites of the Church of England shall be particularly countenanced and encouraged." *

* Compare this with the provisions for the support of the Church, contained in Captain John Mason's Will (1635).

The Rev. Mr. Moodey, the only minister in Portsmouth during the administrations of Cutt and Cranfield, refused to baptize the children of some of his parishioners according to the ceremony of the English Church, though often and earnestly requested. "Liberty of conscience" seems to have been interpreted by him to mean intolerance of any conscience but his own.

Governor Cranfield having obtained leave of absence, quitted the Province on or about the 15th of May, 1685, and was succeeded by his Deputy, Dr. Walter Barefoote. The last-named was superseded, May 25, 1686, by Joseph Dudley, commissioned President of New England (including Massachusetts Bay, Maine, New Hampshire, and the Narragansett or King's Province). Under these two brief administrations but little alteration was made in the statute law of New Hampshire.

Under Governor Andros, whose administration lasted from December 18, 1686, to the 18th of April, 1689, numerous laws, ordinances, and orders were made by the Governor and his Council, but these were chiefly general in their operation. Such of these as have been preserved * are drawn with skill; not a few of them proved beneficial, and some of them were permanently incorporated into the statute laws of the colonies.

During the administrations of Lieutenant-Governors Usher and Partridge, of Governors Allen and the Earl of Bellomont, — that is, between 1692 and 1702, — numerous laws were enacted. The record of fifty-eight of these has been preserved, from which it appears that two were disallowed by the King in Council.

The General Assembly began to print the session laws as early as 1704; but it was not till May 15, 1714, that any steps were taken to have the statute laws revised and codified. In December, 1715, a committee consisting of Col. Richard Gerrish, Joseph Smith, Theodore Atkinson, John Plaisted, Thomas Phipps, and Mark Hunking, Esquires, was appointed to "supervise the laws, and collect them into a body to be printed." The committee had completed their labor by the 6th of February, $17\frac{15}{16}$, and prior to the 5th of April Samuel Penhallow, Treasurer of the Province, had "discoursed the printer," Benjamin Green, of Boston. The title

* Col. Records of Conn. (1679–89), 402–436.

of this, the first printed collection of the laws of the Province, is as follows: —

Acts | and | Laws, | Passed by the | General Court | or | Assembly | Of His Majesties | Province | of | New-Hampshire | in | New-England. | G [Royal Seal] R | Boston in New-England: | Printed by B. Green: Sold by Eleazar Russel | at his Shop in Portsmouth. 1716. |

This volume, known as Russell's edition, covers 60 folio pages, besides the title-page. In 1718, there were added 72 pages of laws, and a table of contents, 4 pages; in 1719, the laws passed May 2, of that year, 24 pages;* in 1722, the laws passed in 1721, being 7 pages, and a table of contents, 8 pages, covering all the laws printed up to that date; and in 1726, the laws passed in 1722, '24, '25, being 8 pages, or a total of 124 pages printed subsequently to 1716. By an error of the printer, the pagination of folios 157–163 is repeated. The whole number of pages in the few copies of this volume still extant is 184.

Among the laws enacted in 1718 was one that authorized the Judge of Probate, for the Province, to license executors and administrators to sell so much of the realty as was necessary to pay the debts and legacies. By this great step forward New Hampshire anticipated the action of Massachusetts, in this matter, nearly one hundred years.

---

* The following is Treasurer Penhallow's account of the expense of Printing these 24 pages:—

"Province of New-Hampshire Dr
To printing the Last Sett of Laws
w[ch] was in Sep[r] Last—

viz[t]:

To my going to Boston & Carying y[e] Laws	5: — —
To five Rheem of Paper at 22s	5: 10: —
To printing of 300 Setts of six Sheets in Each Sett at 24s	7: 4: —
To y[e] Supervisor of y[e] Press	4: — —
To Mr Phipps for his Troble in transcribing Laws since y[e] Last acco[tt]	15: 10: 6
To y[e] Post for his bringing the Laws from Boston—	10:
	£37: 14: 6

Portsm[o]. Apr[ll] 26, 1720.
Err[r]s Excepted

Sam[l] Penhallow"

During the next fifty years frequent attempts were made to obtain a revision of the laws, but nothing was accomplished till 1761. In that year Meshech Weare, — a name soon afterward most honorably connected with the legislative, judicial, and administrative history of the Province and of the State, — was a member of the committee on the laws. This committee reported a revised draft in print. It does not appear that the report was accepted, or acted upon in any particular; and it is reasonable to suppose that this revision did not meet the demands of the Assembly. A few copies of this report have been preserved. The title reads as follows: —

Acts | and | Laws | of | His Majesty's Province | of | New-Hampshire, | in | New-England. | With Sundry Acts of Parliament. | By order of the Governor, | Council and Assembly, | Pass'd October 16th. 1759. | Portsmouth, Printed by Daniel Fowle. | 1761. |

This, known as Fowle's first edition, contains 236 pages of laws, which, with the title-page and table of contents, make a total of 250 pages folio. Bound up and paged consecutively with the foregoing, some copies of this edition have the laws "publish'd the 27th of June, 1765," 4 pages; and 8 pages of laws "past the 15th of June, 1765," "printed by Daniel and Robert Fowle, 1766," with a collection of "Temporary Laws," covering fifty pages (numbered from 1 to 50, inclusive), printed by the Fowles, in 1768.

This edition not being deemed authentic, efforts were made to induce the Assembly to order a fresh revision; but these efforts were unsuccessful until 1770. On the 24th of March of that year, William Parker, Samuel Livermore, Peter Livius, and George Jaffrey, Esquires, were appointed a committee "to collect and print one hundred and fifty setts of all the Acts and Laws of the Province" then in force. This, known as Fowle's second edition, bears the following title: —

Acts and Laws | of | His Majesty's Province | of | New-Hampshire. | In | New-England. | With Sundry Acts of Parliament. | *By Order of the General Assembly.* | To which is prefix'd the | Commissions | of | President John Cuttss, Esq.; | And His Excellency | John Wentworth, Esq.; | Portsmouth, Printed by

Daniel and Robert Fowle, | And Sold at their Office near the State-House. | 1771. |

This, also, is a folio. It contains 150 Perpetual Laws, 15 Acts of Parliament, or 272 pages; and 26 Temporary Laws, paged from 1 to 51, inclusive; which, with title-page, commissions (19 pages), and table of contents (4), make a total of 344 pages. Bound up with the foregoing, some copies have the laws enacted December 16, 1771, and May 28, 1773, and a few of a still earlier date, all paged consecutively with the edition of 1771. In some copies there will also be found, inserted after page 51 of the Temporary Laws, laws of that class passed between December 23, 1771, and February 12, 1774, making 286 pages of Perpetual, and 72 of Temporary Laws.

Russell's edition of 1716 contains all the laws in Fowle's edition of 1771, as far as page 165, inclusive; and the latter contains all that are embraced in the former, except seven. Both the editions of 1716 and 1761 contain the law against high treason, passed in the 13th of Anne; but it is significant of the changed temper of the people, or of the Assembly, that the edition of 1771 has no law on that subject. In 1777, the Assembly enacted a stringent law; but, of course, the crime there specified was not "treason to the Crown."

Pursuant to the favorable response of the Continental Congress, made November 3, 1775, to the suggestion of the New Hampshire Assembly, a Provincial Congress met in Exeter, and on the 21st of December adopted a plan * of temporary government for the "Colony" of New Hampshire. This plan was promulgated on the 5th of January, 1776, and thus New Hampshire has the distinction of being the first colony or province to adopt a constitution after the outbreak of the Revolutionary War.†

In the preamble to this constitution the Congress declared, —

> "That we never sought to throw off our Dependence upon Great Britain, but felt Ourselves happy under her Protection, while we could enjoy our Constitutional Rights and Privileges. And that we shall rejoice if such a Reconciliation between us and our Parent State can be effected as shall be approved by the Continental Congress."

* Laws of New Hampshire, printed in 1780; Farmer and Moore's His. Col., I., 269-272.

† This temporary government lasted from January 5, 1776, to June 10, 1784.

In the spirit of this declaration the Assembly refused to make any changes in the statute laws, further than the exigencies of the situation required.

Soon after this, doubts having arisen whether their assumption of government, and adoption of the Declaration of Independence, did not operate to vacate the laws in force prior to 1776, the Provincial Congress, on the 9th of April, 1777, passed an Act to reëstablish the general system of laws previously in force, except such as were repugnant to, or incompatible with, the new government, or the laws enacted to carry it into effect.

In 1779 it was ordered that the laws which had been enacted by the provisional government should be printed. Accordingly, a volume containing nearly all the laws passed between March 21, 1776, and April 29, 1780, was issued from the press of Zachariah Fowle, of Exeter, under the oversight of Noah Emery, Esquire, clerk of the House of Representatives. This volume contains 235 pages of laws, which, with the title-page, table of contents (4), and the new "Form of Government" (4), makes a total of 245 pages folio. The title is as follows: —

Acts | and | Laws | of the | State * | of | New-Hampshire, | in | *America.* | By Order of the General Assembly. | To which is prefixed, the | Resolution of the *American* Congress, | For Establishing a Form of Government | in New-Hampshire; | And the | Resolve of the *Provincial* Congress, | For taking up Government in Form. | With the | Declaration | of | *Independence.* | America: | Printed at Exeter, in the State of | New-Hampshire. | M.DCC.LXXX. |

On the 26th of February, 1778, the Assembly voted to call a State convention for the purpose of forming a permanent government. This convention met in Concord on the 10th of June. At a subsequent session, held June 5, 1779, a constitution was agreed upon and submitted to the people, by whom it was rejected. At another convention, held on the first Tuesday of June, 1781, the previous draft was amended, and this was sent to the people, and by them rejected. A third and successful attempt was made in 1783. This constitution went into effect June 10, 1784;

* This style was adopted 11 September, 1776.

and, with the exception of some slight alteration, in 1791 and in 1850, it has remained to this day a monument of the practical good sense of the people of New Hampshire in 1784.

On the 12th of June, 1784, the Hon. Samuel Livermore, chief-justice, Josiah Bartlett, and John Sullivan, Esquires, were appointed a committee to revise the laws. On the 30th of January, 1789, an order was adopted to print all the laws passed subsequently to July, 1776, and John Pickering and Daniel Humphreys, Esquires, were designated to supervise the press, and determine "how many, and what laws should be printed." This collection was printed and issued early in 1789, with the following title: —

The | Perpetual Laws | of the | *State* of *New-Hampshire,* | from the | Session of the General Court, July, 1776, | to the | Session in December 1788, | continued into the present year 1789, | Compiled and Arranged to the Wishes of | the Gentlemen of the Law, and under | the Direction of the General Court. | *Printed from attested copies of the original Acts.* | Misera Servitus est, ubi jus est *vagum* aut *Incognitum.* | Portsmouth: New-Hampshire, printed by John | Melcher, M,DCC,LXXXIX. |

This revision, known among the old lawyers as the "Horn-book," — so called, it is said, from the hardness of the cover, — is a volume of 256 pages octavo.

Prior to the 3d of February, 1789, the law regulating the distribution of intestate estates had followed the Mosaic law in giving a double share to the eldest son. By the revised law, enacted on that day, it was provided that the inheritance shall descend in equal shares among the children, and the legal representatives of such as are dead; and in case of failure of children, shall descend equally among the next of kin, in equal degree, and those who represent them. In June following, the General Court of Massachusetts passed a similar law.

In January, 1790, Jeremiah Smith, Nathaniel Peabody, and John Samuel Sherburne, Esquires, were appointed a committee to collect and revise the laws. Their report was adopted in February, 1791, again revised and amended in January, 1792, and ordered to be printed. In the following June an order was adopted suspending the revised laws till September 15, 1792, with the exception of a few which were suspended till February 1, 1793. On the 20th of June, 1792, an Act was passed which repealed nearly all the statutes enacted prior to the adoption of this revised code. The edition of 1792 was the chief basis of the Statute Law down to near the close of the year 1842. This is an octavo volume of 396 pages, the title of which is as follows:—

The | Laws | of the | State of New-Hampshire, | together with | the Declaration of Independence: | the | Definitive Treaty of Peace | between the | United States of America | and His | Britannic Majesty: | the Constitution of New-Hampshire, | and | the Constitution of the United States, | with its Proposed Amendments. | * * * | Portsmouth: Printed by John Melcher. | 1792. |

A new edition, comprising all the laws then in force, was published in 1797, under the supervision of Nathaniel Adams, Esquire, author of the "Annals of Portsmouth." This an octavo of 492 pages, with the following title:—

The | Laws | of the | State of New-Hampshire, | the | Constitution | of the | *State* of *New-Hampshire,* | and the | Constitution of the United States, | with its Proposed Amendments. | Printed by Order of the Honorable the General-Court. | *State* of *New-Hampshire:* | Portsmouth:— | Printed by John Melcher, | Printer to the State. | 1797. |

The next edition, published in 1805, comprised all the laws then in force, with an Appendix containing sundry repealed statutes, and the census of 1790 and 1800. This is a volume of 531 pages octavo. It was compiled, arranged, and indexed by Jeremiah Smith, Esquire, and printed in Dover by Samuel Bragg, Jr.

In 1815 a still more complete edition was published under the supervision of Jeremiah Smith, then chief-justice, John P. Hale, and Moses Hodgden, Esquires, who were selected by a committee of the legislature, of which the Hon. George Sullivan was chairman. This volume contains a large portion of the repealed statutes, with valuable notes by Judge Smith, and abstracts of the census of the State for 1790, 1800, and 1810. It is an octavo of 668 pages.

The | Laws | of the | State of New-Hampshire; | with the | Constitutions | of the | United States and of the State prefixed. | to which is added | an Appendix, | containing the Declaration of Independence, and such of | the repealed laws as are necessary to be known. | Published by Authority. | Exeter: | Printed by C. Norris & Co., for the State. | 1815.

Under the authority of the Legislature, Judge Smith began in 1815 to publish the session laws, commencing with that year, and such of the repealed statutes as he judged necessary to be known. In 1821, all the laws passed between the June session of 1815 and the June session of 1821, inclusive, and abstracts of the State census of 1790, 1800, 1810, and 1820, were bound into one volume, with a title page which purports to have been printed by Norris & Co., aforesaid, in Exeter, in 1815. This volume is numbered II. in the title, the Revised Statutes of 1815 being reckoned number I., as it would appear.

In 1822, the Probate Laws were revised, under Legislative authority, by the Hon. Charles H. Atherton, John Harris, and James Bartlett, Esquires. Revisions of other portions of the statutes were made in 1827, 1828, and 1829, under authority, by Chief Justice William A. Richardson, John Porter and Samuel D. Bell, Esquires. These revised laws, together with the unrevised (excepting one) were included in the volume published in 1830, by Isaac Long, Jr., in Hopkinton, but printed in Concord by Luther Roby. This is an octavo of vii. and 623 pages.

The | Laws | of the | State of New-Hampshire; | with the | Constitutions | of the | United States and of the State prefixed. | Published by Authority. | Hopkinton: | Published by Isaac Long, Jr. | Luther Roby, Printer. | 1830. |

In 1840, Chief-Justice Joel Parker, Samuel D. Bell, and Charles J. Fox, Esquires, were appointed commissioners to revise, amend, and codify the statute laws. The Chief-Justice did not act. The other commissioners made their report to the Legislature in June, 1842. This was ordered to be printed, and further consideration of the report was deferred to the November session. At that session, after amendment, the report was adopted on the 23d of December. This revision was printed in Concord, by

Carroll & Baker, in 1842, and is a volume of xv. and 555 pages octavo.

The | Revised Statutes | of the | State of New Hampshire, | passed December 23, 1842. | To which are prefixed | the Constitutions | of the United States and of the State of New Hampshire. | Published by order of the Legislature. | [Seal] | Concord: | Published by Carroll & Baker, State Printers. | 1843. |

By authority of the Legislature, conferred in 1852, Ralph Metcalf, Calvin Ainsworth, and Samuel H. Ayer, Esquires, compiled the existing laws under appropriate heads in chapters. They made a partial report in 1852, and a full report in 1853. This is a volume of xvi. and 760 octavo pages. It was printed in 1853, in Concord, by Butterfield & Hill, State printers.

The | Compiled Statutes | of the | State of New Hampshire: | to which are prefixed | the Constitutions | of the | United States and of the State of New Hampshire. | Published by order of the Legislature. | [Seal] | Concord: | Butterfield & Hill, State Printers. | 1853. |

In August, 1865, the Hons. Samuel D. Bell, Asa Fowler, and George Y. Sawyer, were appointed commissioners to revise, amend and codify the statute laws. They were also instructed to supply appropriate marginal notes and citations of adjudicated cases. Their report, after having been amended by a Committee of the Legislature, was adopted in 1867, and makes a volume of xvii. and 676 octavo pages, which was printed in Manchester in 1867, by John B. Clarke, State printer.

The | General Statutes | of the | State of New-Hampshire; | to which are prefixed the | Constitutions of the United States and of the State. | With a Glossary and Digested Index. | [Seal] | Manchester: | John B. Clarke, State Printer. | 1867. |

By this last revision and codification, which is said to be satisfactory in most respects, there was accomplished in New Hampshire, after the lapse of nearly two hundred years from the institution of a lawful and general government, that which a learned and wise statesman, writing about two centuries ago, declared to be a "work worthy of a parliament, and cannot be done otherwise,—

to cause a review of all our statutes, to repeal such as they shall judge inconvenient to remain in force; to confirm those which they shall think fit to stand, and those several statutes which are confused, some repugnant to others, many touching the same matters, to be reduced into certainty, all of one subject into one statute, that perspicuity and clearness may appear in written laws."

Besides the State Constitution, the statutes enacted by the Legislature, and the common law of the State, the people of New Hampshire are subject to the Constitution of the United States, to all treaties made under the authority of the same, and to the laws of Congress.

The Common Law of England and the statutes of Parliament in amendment of it, so far as they were applicable to the circumstances of the country, were in force in New Hampshire from the first settlement. And, because it was a Royal Province, from that time down to the actual acknowledgment of American Independence neither the people by popular vote, nor royal governors or presidents, nor public assemblies, nor any usurping power could lawfully do any act that might operate in any degree as an abridgment or suspension or extinction of the sovereignty of the Crown; nor during any moment was that sovereignty ceded or withdrawn.

www.ingramcontent.com/pod-product-compliance
Lightning Source LLC
LaVergne TN
LVHW020635110826
845149LV00004B/1209

* 9 7 8 1 4 1 8 1 9 1 6 1 0 *